All About

CAMERAS

Amazing photography and film-making

Chris Oxlade and Al Morrison

CONSULTANT John Freeman

southwater

This edition is published by Southwater

Southwater is an imprint of Anness Publishing Ltd
Hermes House, 88–89 Blackfriars Road, London SE1 8HA
tel. 020 7401 2077; fax 020 7633 9499
www.southwaterbooks.com; info@anness.com

© Anness Publishing Ltd 2000, 2003

UK agent: The Manning Partnership Ltd, 6 The Old Dairy
Melcombe Road, Bath BA2 3LR; tel. 01225 478444; fax 01225 478440
sales@manning-partnership.co.uk

UK distributor: Grantham Book Services Ltd, Isaac Newton Way
Alma Park Industrial Estate, Grantham, Lincs NG31 9SD
tel. 01476 541080; fax 01476 541061; orders@gbs.tbs-ltd.co.uk

North American agent/distributor: National Book Network
4501 Forbes Boulevard, Suite 200, Lanham, MD 20706
tel. 301 459 3366; fax 301 429 5746; www.nbnbooks.com

Australian agent/distributor: Pan Macmillan Australia, Level 18
St Martins Tower, 31 Market St, Sydney, NSW 2000; tel. 1300 135 113
fax 1300 135 103; customer.service@macmillan.com.au

New Zealand agent/distributor: David Bateman Ltd, 30 Tarndale Grove
Off Bush Road, Albany, Auckland; tel. (09) 415 7664; fax (09) 415 8892

A CIP catalogue record for this book is available from
the British Library.

Publisher: Joanna Lorenz
Managing Editor, Children's Books: Gilly Cameron Cooper
Project Editor: Joanne Hanks
Consultants: Peter Mellett, John Freeman
Photographer: John Freeman
Stylist and Picture Researcher: Marion Elliot
Designers: Caroline Reeves, Ann Samuel
Illustrators: Richard Hawke, Caroline Reeves,
Clive Spong
Cover design: Joyce Mason

Previously published as *Investigations: Cameras*

1 3 5 7 9 10 8 6 4 2

The publishers would like to thank the following pupils from Hampden
Gurney School: Gary Cooper, Diane Cuffe, Sheree Cunningham-Kelly,
Louisa El-Jonsafi, Sarah Ann Kenna, Lee Knight, Shadae Lawrence,
Robert Nunez, Kim Peterson, Paul Snow, Kisanet Tesfay. They would
also like to thank Keith Johnson and Pelling Ltd for the loan of props.

All About
CAMERAS

CONTENTS

YOU AND YOUR CAMERA

What is the one vital piece of equipment you must not forget if you are on vacation or having a birthday party? Your camera! To most people, a camera is simply a device for taking snapshots of their favorite places and people. Cameras are really sophisticated machines that make use of the latest breakthroughs in science and technology. A camera is designed to do a specific job. It makes a copy of a scene on film by collecting light from that scene and turning it into a picture. It works in a very similar way to your eyes, but it makes a permanent record of the scene instead of simply looking at it.

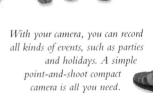

As simple as blinking
Using a camera is like looking through a special window. Blink your eyes. This is how a camera records light from a scene. A shutter opens to let light pass through a glass lens and fall onto the film.

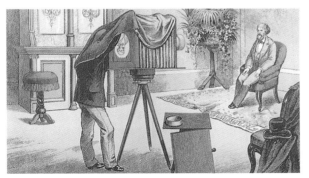

With your camera, you can record all kinds of events, such as parties and holidays. A simple point-and-shoot compact camera is all you need.

Early cameras
The first practical cameras with film were developed in the 1830s. Today, cameras do the same job but are much easier to use. In the early days, it could take half an hour to take a photo. Modern cameras have much shorter exposure time. Scenes can be recorded in a fraction of a second.

Producing prints

A camera is useless without film inside to record the images the lens makes. If you want prints, then the film is developed, or processed to produce negatives. Prints are then made from the negatives and can be enlarged to a variety of different sizes. Frame numbers and details of the type of film used appear on the edge of the strip. The notches are for the use of the processing mini-lab. You can see which of the negatives on this strip produced the print next to it.

negative

print

The winning picture

If professional photographers are shooting a sports or news event, they must get a clear image. Their pictures appear in magazines and newspapers and help us to understand the story.

Professionals at work

These professional photographers are using telephoto lenses to get a closer picture of the event they are recording. Professionals need to use sophisticated equipment and usually carry two or three cameras, a selection of lenses, a tripod, a flash and rolls of film of different speeds.

WHAT IS A CAMERA?

All cameras, from disposable to professional models, have the same basic parts. The camera body is really just a light-proof box. This keeps the light-sensitive film in complete darkness. A section of film is held flat in the back of the body. At the front of the body is the lens, which collects light from the scene and shines it onto the film. Between the lens and the film is a shutter. When you take a photograph, the shutter opens to let light come through the lens onto the film. Many cameras have additional features that help you to take better photographs. In some cameras, the shutter timing and lens position are automatically adjusted to suit different conditions.

Disposable cameras come with the film already inside. You take the whole camera to the film processor when the film is finished.

Compact camera
A compact camera is a small camera that will fit in your pocket. With many models, all you have to do is aim at the scene and press the shutter release button. Simple compacts are also called point-and-shoot cameras.

shutter release button

viewfinder

flash unit, to light up dark scenes

115

viewfinder

pressure plate in camera back keeps film flat

lens protected by plastic flap when camera is not in use

space for roll of film

spool—used film is wound here

Inside the camera
You open the back of the camera to load and unload the film. There is space for the film cassette and a spool where the used film is stored. The film is advanced, or wound, either by an electric motor or by hand.

Close-up care

The view that you see in the viewfinder of a compact camera is not quite the same as the view that the lens sees. This is because the viewfinder is higher up than the lens. Remember to leave some space around close-up objects in the viewfinder.

lens view

viewfinder view

You look through a viewfinder to see what will be in your photo. The guidelines you see in many viewfinders (seen in red here) show you what area of the scene will be included in your picture. If the photographer takes this picture, the boy's hat will be cut off.

Instant photos

Polaroid cameras use special film that produces prints almost instantly.

SLR camera

Focusing on an image

Most modern 35-mm cameras (those needing 35-mm format film) use a single-lens reflex (SLR) design. When you look into the viewfinder, you see exactly what the lens sees. You can change the lens of an SLR camera to achieve different effects.

HOW A LENS WORKS

Making your own simple viewer will show you just how a camera lens collects light from a scene and makes a small copy of it on the film. The copy is called an image. Just like a real camera, the viewer has a light-proof box. At the front of the box is a pin-hole, which works like a tiny lens. The screen at the back of the box is where the film would be in a real camera. This kind of viewer is sometimes called a camera obscura (which just means a dark box used to capture images of outside objects). In the past, artists used these to make images of scenes that they could paint.

MATERIALS

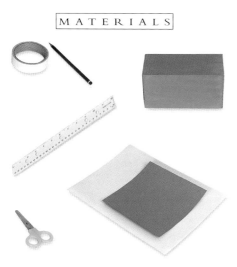

You will need: ruler, scissors, small cardboard box, card stock, sharp pencil, tape, tracing paper.

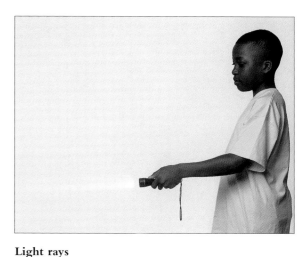

Light rays
Light travels in straight rays. You can see this when you shine a flashlight. When you look at a scene, your eyes collect rays that are coming from every part of it. This is just what a camera does.

MAKE YOUR OWN VIEWER

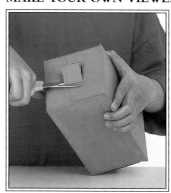

1 Using scissors, cut a small hole, about ½ by ½ in., in one end of the cardboard box.

2 Now cut a much larger square hole in the other end of your cardboard box.

3 Cut a square of card stock 1½ by 1½ in. Pierce a tiny hole in the center with a sharp pencil.

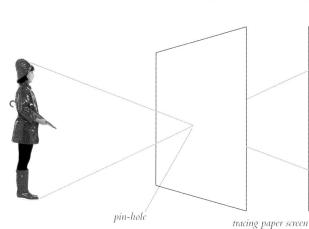

pin-hole

tracing paper screen

If you look at a person through your viewer, light rays from their head hit the bottom of the viewer's screen. Rays from their feet hit the top of the screen. So the screen image is upside down. Left and right are swapped, too.

Making an image with light

When you use your viewer, the pin-hole lets in just a few light rays from each part of the scene. The rays keep going in straight lines and hit the tracing paper screen, making an image of the scene.

A camera obscura

Some camera obscuras are more like rooms than boxes, but they work in the same way. Light from a small hole or simple lens creates a reversed and upside down image on a flat surface. This can be seen in the darkened interior of the room.

6 Now look out of a window, through the screen of tracing paper. Try tracing the image you see on to the paper.

4 Place the card stock over the box's smaller hole. Make sure that the pin-hole is centered over the hole. Now tape it into place.

5 Cut a square of tracing paper slightly bigger than the larger hole. Tape it securely over that hole. Your viewer is ready to use.

EXPERIMENT WITH LIGHT

You will need: ruler, two pieces of card stock, scissors, flashlight, glass of water, magnifying glass, mirror.

L ight is refracted and reflected inside cameras by lenses and mirrors. The best way to see how this happens is to send some light beams through lenses and then bounce them off mirrors yourself. You can make narrow light beams by shining a flashlight through slots in a sheet of card stock. Try these experiments and then see if you have any ideas of your own. Vary the size of the slots to see how the light beams change. Carry out the experiments in a room with the lights off and the blinds or curtains closed.

Converging light rays
The lens of a magnifying glass makes light rays from objects converge, or bend inward, toward each other. So, when the rays enter the eye, they seem to have come from a bigger object.

HAVING FUN WITH BEAMS

1 Cut a slot about ⅛ in. wide and 2 in. long in two pieces of card stock. Bend the bottom edges so they stand up. Shine the light beam of a flashlight through both.

2 To see how the beam can be refracted put a glass of water in its path. Move the glass from side to side to see how the beam widens and narrows.

3 Replace the second piece of card stock with one with three slots in it. Put a magnifying glass in the path of the three beams to make them converge, or bend inward.

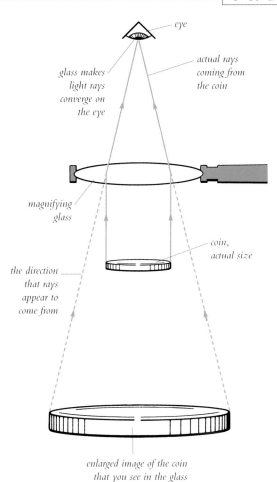

eye

glass makes
light rays
converge on
the eye

actual rays
coming from
the coin

magnifying
glass

coin,
actual size

the direction
that rays
appear to
come from

enlarged image of the coin
that you see in the glass

Water mirror

Unlike other cameras, single-lens reflex cameras (SLRs) give crisp, clean images. To see why, try this simple experiment. Hold a glass of water up so that you can see the bottom surface of the water clearly. Now poke your finger into the water from above. You should see a clear, single reflection of your finger in the surface. This is because the surface acts just like a mirror *(now see box below)*.

4 Now try each of the experiments, but put a mirror in the way of the different beams. Can you see how the pattern of rays stays the same?

MIRRORS AND PRISMS

Stopping reflections

If you look carefully at a reflection in a normal mirror, you will see a "ghostly" second image. The water mirror above does not make a "ghostly" image. To keep from getting "ghostly" images on your pictures, the SLR has a glass block called a pentaprism (a five-angled prism), which treats reflections in the same way as the water mirror.

The same view

The pentaprism in an SLR camera also makes sure that the image you see in the viewfinder is exactly the same as the image on your developed photo.

COMING INTO FOCUS

Before taking a photograph, you need to make sure that your subject is in focus. When it is, all the rays of light that leave a point on the subject are bent by the lens so that they hit the same place on the film. This makes a clear, sharp image on the film. Parts of the scene in front or behind the subject will not be in focus. On some cameras you have to choose the part of the scene that you want to be in focus yourself. Autofocus cameras focus the lens by automatically choosing the object at the center of the focal plane.

In this photograph (above), the subject is in sharp focus. You can see all the fine detail. When the same shot is out of focus (below), it makes the subject look blurred.

focal plane

The focal plane
When the image of a subject is in focus, the light rays meet on the film focal plane. The camera's film is held flat in the focal plane by a pressure plate, visible if you open the back of your (empty) camera.

pentaprism

viewfinder

lens

light ray

mirror

Focusing SLRs
With an SLR camera, you see exactly what the image looks like through the viewfinder. On a manual-focus SLR, you turn a ring around the lens to get your subject in focus.

Getting closer
Use a magnifying glass and lamp to make an image of an object on a sheet of paper. Move the magnifying glass closer to and farther away from the paper, to bring different parts of the scene into focus.

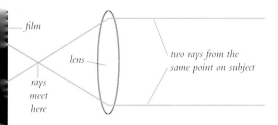

The lens, here, is too far away from the film. Rays from the subject meet in front of the film, so it is out of focus.

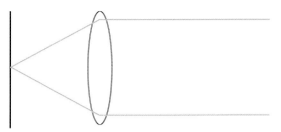

To focus, the lens is moved backward, toward the film. The rays now meet on the film.

In and out of focus

A camera focuses on a subject by moving the lens backward and forward so it gets closer to, or farther away from the film. This brings parts of the scene that are at different distances from the camera into focus. When the lens is set closest to the film, objects from the distance are in sharper focus.

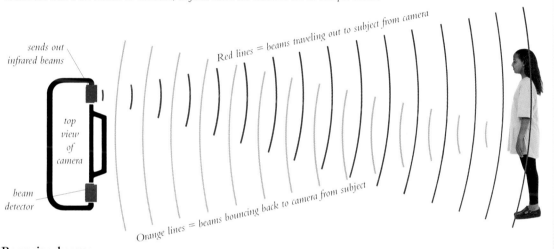

sends out infrared beams

Red lines = beams traveling out to subject from camera

top view of camera

beam detector

Orange lines = beams bouncing back to camera from subject

Bouncing beams

With the type of autofocus system shown here, the camera emits a wide beam of invisible infrared light. It figures out how long the infrared light takes to bounce back, and so knows how far away the subject is. A small electric motor then moves the lens.

Autofocus errors

Most autofocus cameras focus on objects that are in the center of the scene in the viewfinder. If your subject is off to one side, the camera focuses on the background, and your subject will be blurred *(left)*. If you have a focus lock, you can prevent this by aiming at the subject first, and then using your focus lock before recomposing the shot and shooting *(right)*.

MAKE YOUR OWN CAMERA

You will need: pin-hole box viewer, aluminum foil, scissors, tape, pencil, black paper, thin card stock, thick cloth or plastic, photographic paper, rubber band.

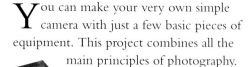

Y ou can make your very own simple camera with just a few basic pieces of equipment. This project combines all the main principles of photography. For simplicity, this camera uses photographic paper (paper with a light-sensitive coating on one side) instead of film and a pin-hole instead of a lens. When the "film" (paper) is processed, you will have a negative. Then turn to the "Printing and Projecting" project to find out how you can make a print from the negative. Find out about the equipment you need in the "Recording an Image" project.

MAKING A PIN-HOLE CAMERA

1 Make the pin-hole viewer from the "How a Lens Works" project, but remove the tracing-paper screen. Replace the 1½-in. card stock square with aluminum foil. Pierce a hole, about ⅛ in. across, in the center of the foil using a sharp pencil.

2 Open the back of the box and line the inside with black paper. Alternatively, color the inside with a black felt-tip pen.

3 Cut a square of card stock large enough to cover the aluminum foil. Tape just the top edge to the box, so that it will act as a shutter.

4 Cut a square of card stock to fit right across the other end of the box. Tape it to one edge so that it closes over the hole like a door or flap.

5 Find some heavy, black, light-proof cloth or a plastic sheet. Cut a piece large enough to fold around the end of the box.

6 In a completely dark room, feeling with your fingers, put a piece of photographic paper under the flap at the end of the box.

7 Close the flap, then wrap the cloth or plastic sheet tightly over it. Next, put rubber band tightly around the box to secure it.

8 Now you can turn the light on. Point the camera at a well-lit object and open the shutter. Leave the camera still for about five minutes and then close the shutter.

Disposable camera
Single use cameras have the film already loaded and ready to use. You send the whole camera when you want the film to be developed.

Opening the shutter allows light to strike the piece of light-sensitive paper. The paper is coated to turn dark where light strikes it. This gives you a negative, on paper instead of on film. Next, you need to develop the image on the paper with developing fluid (see the "Printing and Projecting" project). This will give you the negative image on the sheet of paper as it appears here.

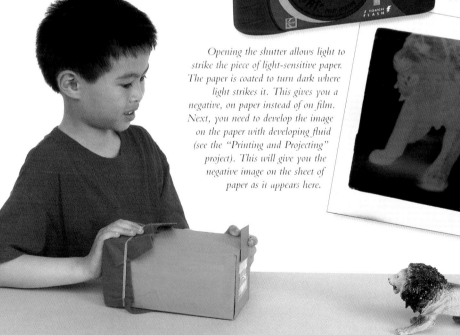

USING FILM

The camera's job is to create a focused image of a scene, but this would be no use without a way of recording the image. This is the job of the film. Film is coated with a type of silver that is affected by light. So when an image strikes the film, the silver records the patterns of light, dark and color. You cannot look at film right away. It must be developed first with chemicals that turn the silver black or gray where light has struck it. Until then, it must be kept in complete darkness. If undeveloped film is exposed to direct light, it turns completely black.

Always load and unload film in dim light or in shadow, to prevent light from leaking into the film canister.

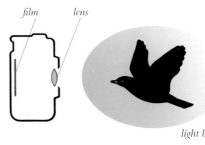

film   *lens*

The film is exposed by the camera when you photograph something, such as this bird against a light background (left).

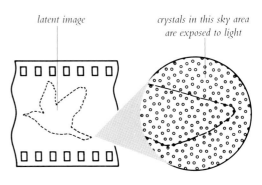

latent image   *crystals in this sky area are exposed to light*

Crystals in the light area of the image change. Crystals in the dark area do not. The image has been recorded chemically. Nothing shows up on the film, and the image is called the latent (hidden) image.

Types of film

There are several different types of film. The one most people use is film for color prints. This is called color negative film. Other common types are black-and-white negative film for making black-and-white positive prints and color reversal film for making slides.

Exposing a film

Black-and-white film contains millions of microscopic light-sensitive crystals that contain silver. When a photograph is taken, some of the crystals that are exposed to light begin to break down, leaving silver metal. In the areas where more light falls, more crystals begin to change.

Processing film

Amateur photographers develop black-and-white film at home, in a small developing tank. In the dark, the film is wound carefully onto a plastic spiral. The spiral is then placed in the tank and a lid is put on. A chemical called developer is poured into the tank and left for a few minutes before being poured out. Then chemical fixer is poured in. Finally, the film is washed.

Film drying

After washing, film is carefully dried. They are usually hung up to dry in a dust-free area, sometimes in a special drying cabinet. Once the film is dry, the photographer can cut it into manageable strips and choose which ones to print.

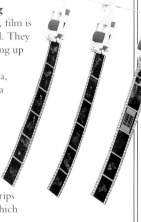

black background with white bird

changed crystals

unchanged crystals

During developing (above), all the crystals that had begun to break down change completely to silver. They look black. The unchanged crystals stay as they are.

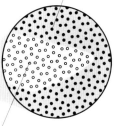

black background with clear bird

changed crystals

no crystals

Fixing gets rid of all the unchanged crystals, leaving clear film. The result is a negative, where dark areas on the original subject are light, and light areas are dark.

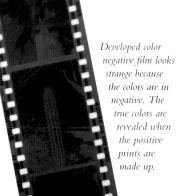

Developed color negative film looks strange because the colors are in negative. The true colors are revealed when the positive prints are made up.

When color reversal, or slide film, is developed, the actual colors of the scene are reproduced as a positive image.

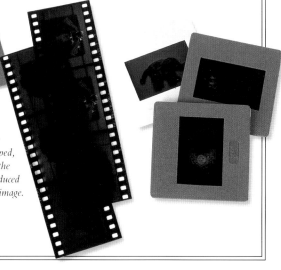

THE RIGHT FILM

There are three basic types of film. They are color negative film, color-reversal film and black–and–white film. Film comes in different sizes (called formats). Most cameras use 35-mm film, which comes in a preloaded container called a cassette. Film also comes in different lengths. The lengths are measured by the number of exposures, or photographs, that will fit on the film. The usual lengths are 24 and 36 exposures. You also have to decide which speed of film to use. Fast film reacts to light more quickly than slow film. Film speed is referred to by its ISO (International Standards Organization) rating. The most common speeds are ISO 100 and ISO 200, which are medium-speed films.

Automatic coding
On one side of a film cassette is a pattern of black and silver squares. This is called a DX code and it indicates the film's ISO rating and length. Modern cameras have sensors that can read the code and display it in the viewfinder. On older cameras, you have to set the ISO rating manually on a dial.

All the details of a film (format, speed and length) are printed on the film carton and the film cassette. The carton also has an expiration date.

Which film speed?
The difference between films of different speeds is the size of their crystals (or grains). Fast film (ISO 400 and above) is perfect for shooting in dim light and for action shots (or when the subject won't sit still). They have larger grains than slow films. This is because larger grains can react to much less light than small ones. These large grains often show up in the final picture *(above right)*. Slow films (ISO 50 and below) are perfect for fine, crisp detail *(above left)*.

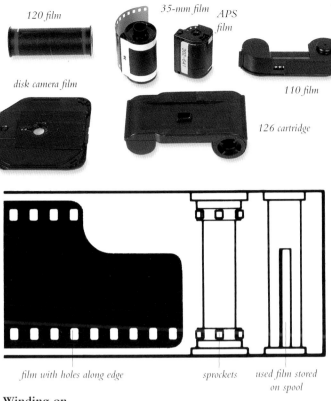

120 film

35-mm film

APS film

disk camera film

110 film

126 cartridge

film with holes along edge *sprockets* *used film stored on spool*

Film and photo formats

Format is the size of the film and the size and shape of each image recorded on the film. Large-format films give much more detail. Smaller formats are more convenient. Some cameras can take photographs of different formats on the same film using adapters or masks.

Indoor film

Most color film is designed for use in daylight. If you use it indoors, with light from lightbulbs, the photos come out yellowy. You can buy indoor film called tungsten film, which gives the right colors, or use a conversion filter that compensates for indoor light.

Winding on

35-mm and APS (Advanced Photographic System) film have small holes along each side. The holes fit over sprockets in the camera that turn to wind on the film. This brings a fresh part of unexposed film behind the lens. Roll films have backing paper that shields the film from stray light. This film is wound from one spool to another as it is exposed.

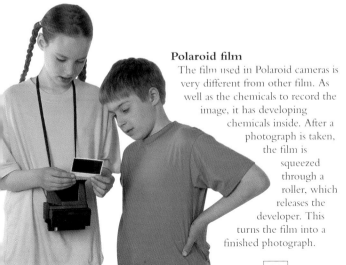

Polaroid film

The film used in Polaroid cameras is very different from other film. As well as the chemicals to record the image, it has developing chemicals inside. After a photograph is taken, the film is squeezed through a roller, which releases the developer. This turns the film into a finished photograph.

FACT BOX

• Infrared film is coated with chemicals that react to heat, rather than to the visible light rays, coming from a scene.

• The largest negative that has ever been used measured 21 by 1 ft. This massive negative was made for a huge panoramic picture of 3,500 people, photographed in the United States in 1992.

• 35-mm format film was originally developed for movie cameras. It is still the most common format for movie camera film.

RECORDING AN IMAGE

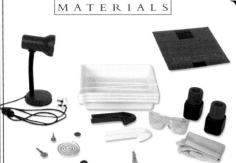

You will need: lamp, photographic paper, different-shaped objects such as keys, disks and scissors, rubber gloves, protective goggles, plastic tongs, plastic dishes, chemicals (see below).

You do not need a camera to see how film works. In fact you do not need film either! You can use black-and-white photographic paper instead. Photographic paper is the paper that prints are made on. It works in the same way as film. Here, you can see how to make a picture called a photogram. It is made by covering some parts of a sheet of photographic paper with objects and then shining light on the sheet. When the paper is developed the areas that were hit by the light turn black, leaving you an image of the objects.

Photographic chemicals

You will need two photographic chemicals: developer for paper (not film) and fixer. Buy them at a photographic supplier. Ask an adult to help you follow the instructions on the bottles to dilute (mix with water) the chemicals, and make sure you protect your eyes and hands when handling them. Store the diluted chemicals in plastic bottles. Seal the bottles and label them clearly.

MAKE YOUR OWN PHOTOGRAM

1 Turn off the light. Lay a sheet of photographic paper down, shiny-side up. Put objects on it. Turn the light on again for a few seconds.

2 Pick up the paper with the tongs and put it into the dish of developer. Push it down so that the paper is under the liquid.

3 After a minute, use the tongs to move the paper into the fixer. Leave it under the liquid for a minute, until the image is set.

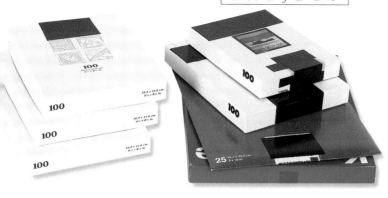

This symbol, on photographic chemical bottles, means that they can be dangerous if not used with care. Always wear gloves and goggles.

Photographic paper

For black-and-white prints, you need paper called monochrome paper. Buy the smallest size you can, and choose grade 2 if possible, with a gloss finish. The paper comes in a light-proof envelope or box. Only open the envelope in complete darkness. The paper is in a second, black plastic envelope.

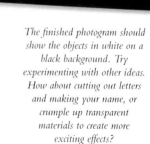

The finished photogram should show the objects in white on a black background. Try experimenting with other ideas. How about cutting out letters and making your name, or crumple up transparent materials to create more exciting effects?

4 Now you can turn the light back on. Using the tongs, lift the paper out of the fixer and wash it with running water for a few minutes. Then lay the paper on a flat surface to dry. This technique is an excellent way of producing unique invitations or greeting cards quickly and effectively.

THE CAMERA SHUTTER

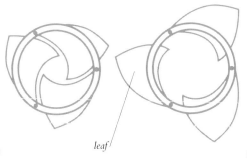

leaf

A leaf shutter has thin metal plates called leaves. These overlap each other to close the shutter (left) and swivel back to open it (right).

All cameras have a shutter between the lens at the front and the film at the back. The shutter is much like a door. It is closed most of the time, so that no light gets to the film. When you press the button to take a photo, the shutter opens briefly and then closes again, to let light from your subject reach the film. The time for which the shutter is open is called the shutter speed. Compact cameras have a leaf shutter close to the lens. SLR cameras, which have interchangeable lenses, have a focal-plane shutter, which is located just in front of the film. You should be careful not to touch the shutter when loading film in this type of camera.

first curtain

Focal-plane shutter

This has two curtains. When the camera takes a photograph, the first curtain opens to let light hit the film. The second curtain follows closely behind, covering up the film again. The smaller the gap between the curtains, the faster the shutter speed.

second curtain

Shutter speeds

Most photographs are taken with a shutter speed of between 1/60 and 1/250 of a second. On some SLR cameras, you have to set the shutter speed by turning a dial *(below)*. Each setting gives a shutter speed about twice as fast as the one before.

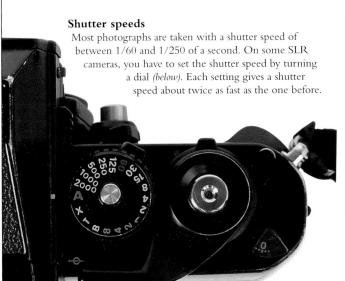

Camera shake

When the shutter is open, even tiny camera movements make the image move across the film, causing a slightly blurred picture. This is called camera shake. It can happen if the shutter speed is below about 1/60 of a second.

A tripod forms a steady base for a camera. It is very useful if you are taking photographs with slow shutter speeds because there is no chance of camera shake. Using a tripod will also help you to compose your pictures really well, because you do not have to worry about holding the camera. You can also vary the height of your viewpoint.

The above picture shows the famous sprinter and long jumper Carl Lewis in action. The photographer has panned the camera (moved it to follow the athlete), which has blurred the background, enhancing the impression of speed. Only Lewis' arms and feet are blurred, which adds to the feeling of action.

Panning, or moving your camera to follow a moving subject, helps to stop the area that is traveling across the frame from being blurred. The stationary elements (background) of the photo will still appear fuzzy.

When you photograph action, such as people running, a fast shutter speed will freeze the action and prevent a blurred shot. Panning will also help, especially if your subject is moving across the scene. To pan, aim at your subject and swing the camera to follow it, squeezing the shutter release button when the subject is where you want it.

There are several ways of keeping your camera steady as you take a photograph, even if you do not have a tripod. For example, stand with your legs slightly apart, or crouch down with one knee on the ground. Squeeze the shutter release button slowly. For extra steadiness, lean against a tree, or try resting your camera on a wall. A friend's shoulder or chair are also good ideas.

WHAT AN APERTURE DOES

The aperture ring on an SLR lens. Aperture size is measured in f-numbers (such as f/8).

The aperture is basically a hole, situated behind the camera lens, that can be made larger or smaller. When the aperture is small, some of the light rays that pass through the lens are cut off so that they do not reach the film. This does not cut off any of the image on the film, but it does reduce the amount of light that hits the film, making the image darker. Changing the size of the aperture also affects how much of the scene is in focus. Some cameras, such as the disposable variety, have a pre-set aperture.

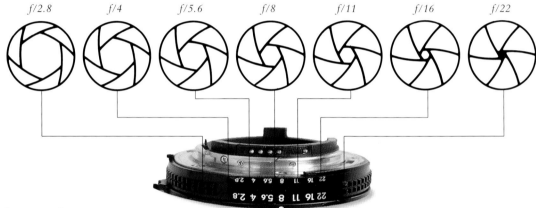

| f/2.8 | f/4 | f/5.6 | f/8 | f/11 | f/16 | f/22 |

Aperture sizes

The mechanism that changes aperture size has interlocking metal leaves. These fold in to make the aperture smaller. The f-number is a fraction—f/4 means a quarter of the focal length of the lens. (Focal length is the distance from the lens to the focal point, where light rays from an object come together.) So an aperture of f/8 is half the width of one of f/4, and lets in one-quarter of the amount of light.

Changing depth of field

Depth of field is the distance between the nearest part of the scene that is in focus and the farthest part of the scene that is in focus. As f-numbers get bigger, the aperture gets smaller and the depth of field increases. Shooting on a sunny day will let you use a small aperture. This makes it easier to get a large depth of field. The depth of field can be set on some cameras.

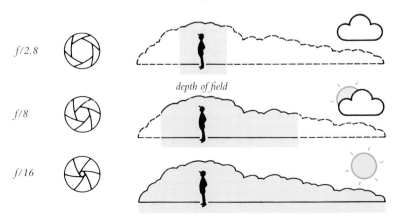

f/2.8

f/8

f/16

depth of field

This photograph was taken with a much smaller aperture than the photograph on the far left, making the depth of field much deeper. Almost everything in the scene is in focus. Greater depth of field is useful for photographs of scenery or architecture where you want to show clear detail. It is also useful if you have people in the foreground and want both the people and the background to be in focus.

In this photograph, the subject (the children) is in focus, and the background is totally out of focus. This is called a shallow depth of field because only the objects that are a certain distance from the camera are in focus. Using shallow depth of field is ideal if you want to make parts of the scene that might confuse your picture disappear into a blur.

FACT BOX

• A lens always has its maximum aperture written on it. For example, a lens described as 300 f/4 has a focal length of 300 mm (12 in.) and a maximum aperture of f/4.

• Large maximum apertures tend to be very expensive because the lenses have to be much bigger. For example, an f/1.4 lens can cost several times as much as an f/4 lens.

• A pin-hole camera the size of a shoe-box has an aperture of about f/500 (1/500th of the focal length).

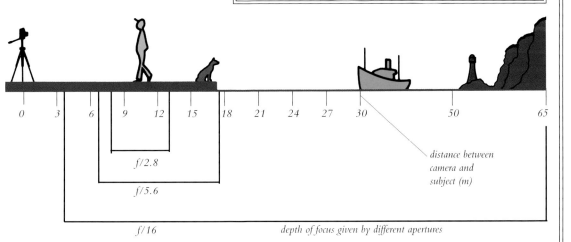

distance between camera and subject (m)

f/2.8

f/5.6

f/16   depth of focus given by different apertures

Try focusing your camera at a certain object and then changing the aperture. You will see how different areas of the picture come into focus.

Lens focused at 9 ft
Aperture at f/2.8
Depth of field=5 ft

Lens focused at 9 ft
Aperture at f/5.6
Depth of field=11½ ft

Lens focused at 9 ft
Aperture at f/16
Depth of field=65 ft

THE RIGHT EXPOSURE

Exposure is the word for the amount of light that reaches the film in your camera when you take a photograph. Exposure depends on the shutter speed (slower shutter speeds give more time and allow more light through) and the aperture (larger apertures also allow more light through). You might see exposure stated on your camera as a combination of shutter speed and aperture—for example, f/16 at 1/60 sec. All but the simplest cameras measure the amount of light coming from the scene and figure out what exposure is needed for the speed of the film in the camera. They do this with an electronic light sensor called a metering system.

In this picture, too little light has reached the film, and the chemicals have not reacted enough. This is called underexposure. The finished photo looks too dark and usually has a grainy quality. Nothing can really be done to improve it in processing.

Here, too much light has reached the film, and the chemicals in the film have reacted too much. This is called overexposure. The final photo is washed out. It can be corrected in printing, unlike underexposure.

When this photograph was taken, the exposure was correct and exactly the right amount of light reached the film. The finished picture is well-balanced—neither too light, nor too dark.

Shutter speed and aperture

Try using different combinations of shutter speed and aperture, each of which lets in the same amount of light *(see right)*, and see what a difference it makes. For example, f/8 at 1/125 sec gives the same amount of light as f4 at 1/500 sec. But a narrower aperture (f8) gives a greater depth of field. You might use the wider aperture (f4) for a fast, action shot and the narrower aperture (f8) for a landscape shot where you want greater depth of field.

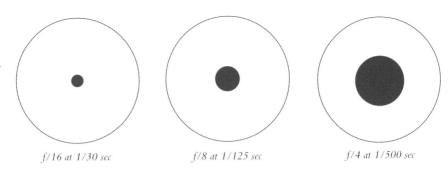

f/16 at 1/30 sec   *f/8 at 1/125 sec*   *f/4 at 1/500 sec*

FACT BOX

• Some cameras can measure the changes in brightness across a scene automatically and then take an average reading for the whole scene.

• There are certain advanced APS (Advanced Photographic System) cameras that can remember the exposure settings for each picture on a roll of film.

• It is more important to get the exposure right if you are using slide (color reversal) film, rather than print film (color negative). This is partly because it is possible to correct mistakes when making prints, but not when making slides.

In the picture on the left, the light shining through the window is brighter than the main subject— the girl. This means that the camera measures more of the light coming from the brighter area. As a result, the background is correctly exposed, but the girl is underexposed and looks too dark.

In this picture, the background was still by far the brightest part of the picture. The problem was solved, however, by using a much larger exposure, and the balance is just right. Bright lighting coming from the background is called backlighting.

LETTING IN THE LIGHT

Changing a camera's aperture affects both the brightness of an image and the depth of field. You can see how it works with a few simple experiments. First, look at your own eyes. Like an aperture, your pupils automatically narrow in bright light to protect your retinas, and open wide to let you see in dim light. To see a shutter at work, open the back of your camera (when there is no film in it). Now look for a leaf shutter near the lens or a focal-plane shutter just behind where the film would be.

MATERIALS

You will need: magnifying glass, cardboard tube, tape, scissors, thin card stock, tracing paper, table lamp, pencil.

Use your eyes
Look closely at one of your eyes in a mirror. Close it and, after a few seconds, open it again quickly. You should see your pupil go from wide to narrow as your eye adjusts to the bright light.

INVESTIGATING APERTURES

1 Carefully attach the magnifying glass to one end of your cardboard tube using small pieces of tape.

2 Roll a piece of thin card stock around the other end of the tube. Tape the top edge down to make another tube that slides in and out.

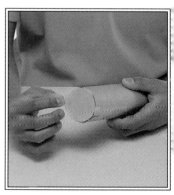

3 With tape, attach a circle of tracing paper across the end of the sliding cardboard tube. This will form your viewing screen.

See a shutter at work

To see just how a shutter works, open the back of your camera (when there is no film inside) and carefully place a small strip of tracing paper where your film usually goes. Now aim the camera at a subject, preferably one that is brightly lit, and press the shutter release button. You should see a brief flash of the image on your tracing paper—although there will be no lasting picture! Be very careful not to put your fingers on the shutter blades in the focal-plane cameras.

4 With the screen nearest to you, aim your tube at a table lamp that is turned on. Can you see an image of the bulb on the screen?

5 Slide the tubes together until the image of the bulb is clear. Now adjust them again so that the image is slightly out of focus.

6 Mark then cut a small hole (about ¼ in. wide) in a piece of card stock, to make a small aperture. Look at the light bulb again and put the card stock in front of the lens. The smaller aperture will bring the light bulb into focus. Is it clearer? Can you read the writing on the bulb?

PRINTING

When film is developed, the images on the film are usually too small to look at. You can view slide films with a projector, which makes a large copy of the image on a screen. But before you can look at photographs taken with negative film, you have to make prints. The paper used for prints is light-sensitive, just like film. To make a print, the negative image is projected onto the paper. When the paper is developed, you get a positive image, so that the scene appears as you saw it originally.

Negatives
When black-and-white film is processed, light areas of the scene appear dark and dark areas appear light. This is a negative.

If you are using black-and-white film, bear in mind that bright areas of the image change the chemicals in the film more than dark areas.

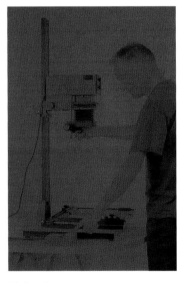

Developing and fixing
The paper is processed in the dark, using chemicals. The three trays hold the developer, water or stop bath (to stop the developer) and fixer. Areas where light has hit the paper come out dark. So light areas of the negative come out dark, as in the original scene.

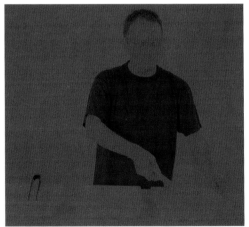

Enlarging
This is the first stage in making a print. An enlarger projects the negative onto paper placed below it. This must be done in the dark, so that no stray light ruins the paper. Lighter areas of the negative allow more light to reach the paper than darker areas.

The final print
After processing, the final print must be dried carefully, to prevent it from getting scratched or curling at the edges. Once developed, take care of your prints by mounting them on card stock using a glue such as photo spray mount. You can then frame your favorite pictures, or keep them in a photograph album.

Printing in color

Color prints are produced in the same way as black–and–white prints. The negative *(above)* is projected onto color photographic paper. When the paper is developed, the colors are reversed once again, so that they come out looking natural.

Color photos

When you take a photo with color negative film, the film records the patterns of color in a scene. When the film is developed, the colors on the film look very strange, but the prints come out correctly. Color film has three layers, one on top of the other. These react to three primary colors, yellow, magenta (blue-red) and cyan (blue-green), which together can produce all of the different colors in the light spectrum.

Processing and printing

Most people send their film to be processed and printed *(above)* by a special photographic laboratory. Some stores, however, have their own automatic processing and printing machines, often called mini-labs. These can produce prints on the spot in a very short period of time.

FACT BOX

• The negative/positive method of photography was invented in 1839 by an Englishman named William Fox Talbot.

• High-contrast printing paper makes blacks look blacker and whites look whiter. Low-contrast paper creates less of a difference between the blacks and the whites.

• Professionals can make parts of a print look lighter or darker by using special techniques on the enlarger. For example, they can "burn" certain areas, which means making more light get to them.

PRINTING AND PROJECTING

If you have just taken a photograph with your own pin-hole camera, you can find out how to turn it into a print below. There is also a simple projector for you to make. A projector lets you look at slide film. On this type of film the colors of the image on the developed film are the same as the colors in the original scene. Projecting a slide is much like the reverse of taking a photograph. First, light is shone through the slide. The light then passes through the lens of the projector and is focused on a flat surface such as a wall, where an enlarged version of the slide appears.

You will need: photographic paper and chemicals, negative from pin-hole camera, flashlight or table lamp, safety goggles, rubber gloves, plastic dishes, plastic tongs or tweezers.

A slide viewer is a special magnifying glass with an opalescent (milky-color) screen used for looking at slides. It is an alternative to a projector. You can also use a light box (a glass box with a light inside) to look at you slides before viewing in a projector.

QUICK AND EASY PRINTS

1 In a totally dark room, lay a fresh sheet of photographic paper on a flat surface, shiny-side up. Lay the negative from your pin-hole camera face-down on top.

2 Shine a flashlight or a table lamp on the top of the two papers for a few seconds. Turn the flashlight off and remove your paper negative. Put on the goggles and gloves.

3 Put the fresh paper into a tray of developing fluid, then fix and wash the fresh paper (see the pages on "Printing"). You should end up with a print of the original image.

DO-IT-YOURSELF PROJECTOR

You will need: cardboard tube, scissors, developed color negative film, thin card stock, tape, magnifying glass, tracing paper, flashlight.

Old projector

This device *(left)* from around 1900 provided a way of looking at color slides. Instead of three layers of color on the film, three separate negatives were taken. Blue, green and red light were projected simultaneously at the same place as the black-and-white slides. The three colors combined to produce the range of colors in the slide scene.

1 Cut two slits on each side of the cardboard tube at one end. They must be wide enough for a strip of negatives to slide through. Only use old negatives that you do not want.

2 Wrap a piece of card stock around the other end of the tube. Tape down the edge to make another tube that slides over the first tube.

3 Tape the magnifying glass to the end of the adjustable tube. Now tape a disk of tracing paper over the slotted end of the main tube.

4 Hold the projector about 6 ft away from a light-colored wall. Slot the negative into the tube and shine a flashlight through it. Adjust the tubes until an image of the negative appears on the wall. You can also try this with slide film, but only use old, unwanted slides.

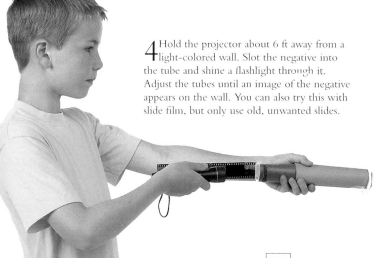

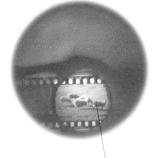

the image as projected on the wall or screen

WIDE AND NARROW

A ll camera lenses have their own focal length, which is written somewhere on the lens. The focal length is the distance between the center of the lens and the focal plane inside the camera where the light coming through the lens creates an image of the object being photographed. Lenses of different focal lengths produce images on the film that contain more or less of a scene. If you use a 50-mm lens, you see the same scene as you do with your eyes. Lenses with shorter focal lengths take in more of the scene, and longer lenses take in less than you would normally see.

What the lens sees

Put your hands on each side of your face. Your view is similar to what a 50-mm lens can see. Keeping your hands the same distance apart, move your hands steadily away from your face. The view between your hands will show you what a telephoto lens sees.

Only light rays that pass through the very center remain straight.

A wide angle lens has a wider angle of view (about 50% more) than the human eye.

Ultra-wide angle

The widest type of lens collects light from a complete half-circle (180 degrees). It makes straight lines appear curved, and the center of the scene seems to bulge outward. It is called a fish-eye lens because fish have eyes that gather light from wide angles.

Long-lens wobble

With telephoto lenses, which have very long focal lengths (300-mm or more), the tiniest bit of camera shake blurs the image. Professionals always use a tripod or monopod with these lenses to keep the camera steady. This is also important because the amount of light that reaches the lens is quite small, and so slow shutter speeds are often needed.

View from a compact camera

The simplest compact cameras usually have a 35-mm lens. This gives a slightly wider view *(left)* than you see with your own eyes. Many compacts now come with a built-in zoom lens enabling you to get a closer shot of your subject while you are still far away from it. These are especially useful for taking portraits (see "Close-up Shots" to find out more).

compact camera with variable lens

the view through a telephoto lens

Telephoto lens view

Any lens that gives you a magnified view of a scene is called a telephoto lens. A telephoto lens is a little like a telescope, because it homes in on just one part of the scene. Telephoto lenses are often used to photograph portraits and distant wildlife, and for coming in close on the small details in a scene.

a wide-angle lens view

Wide-angle lenses

Any camera lens that gives a wider view than we usually see with our eyes is called a wide-angle lens. Extremely wide-angle lenses (of 28-mm and less) allow you to get a huge amount of a scene into your photograph. A really wide-angle lens is perfect to use for panoramic photographs of scenery—such as cityscapes.

CLOSE-UP SHOTS

To keep from having to carry several lenses with different focal lengths, many photographers use one lens, called a zoom lens. These can change their focal length. A zoom lens usually consists of three separate lenses, with adjustable distances between them. They let you change how much of a scene will be in a shot without having to move your body.

A compact camera with a built-in zoom lens. Pressing a button on the camera makes the zoom get longer or shorter.

The built-in lens on many compact cameras, and the lens that comes with most SLRs, is a zoom. A common zoom is 35–70, which means the lens can have focal lengths between 35 mm and 70 mm. It goes from wide angle to short telephoto (which brings objects closer). Macro, or close-up, lenses can focus on things that are very close to the lens. They are ideal for shots of flowers and insects.

Super-zooms
A super-zoom lens has a very large range of focal lengths. For example, a 28–200 zoom goes from very wide angle to long telephoto.

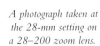

A photograph taken at the 28-mm setting on a 28–200 zoom lens.

SLR zooms
With an SLR and two interchangeable zoom lenses, such as 28–70 and 75–300, you can have a huge range of focal lengths. The focal length is changed by turning or sliding a wide ring on the lens. Because zoom lenses are so complicated, they can make straight lines in a scene look slightly bent, especially at the picture's edges. A special streaked effect can be produced if you zoom in on a subject during a long exposure.

Zooming in for detail with a 200-mm setting.

Close-up equipment
Special high-powered microscope cameras, such as the one on the right, are used for some very close-up shots, such as the close-up of an insect on the left. SLR camera lenses can be removed and replaced with a microscope adapter.

Extension tubes
Extension tubes fit between the camera body and the lens. They move the lens farther from the film. This means that the lens can bend light rays into focus from objects that would usually be too close. A set of extension tubes has three tubes of different lengths for different magnifications.

extension tube

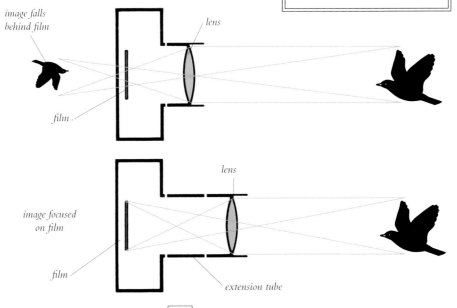

image falls behind film

lens

Usually, the light rays from a close-up object are not bent enough to form a focused image.

film

With an extension tube, the lens moves forward, making room for the rays to become focused.

lens

image focused on film

film

extension tube

FOCAL LENGTHS

If you have either an SLR camera or a compact camera with a zoom lens, then you will probably have taken photographs at different focal lengths. The simple experiments shown on these two pages will help to explain how different focal lengths make more or less of a scene appear on the film. These will help you to give more impact to your pictures. In the mini experiment on the left, try to find as many convex lenses as you can to experiment with. You will find that weaker lenses, which have longer focal lengths, make larger images. This is the opposite to what happens if you use them as a magnifying glass.

Working with lenses
Standing by a window, use a magnifying glass to form an image of the window on a piece of paper. See what happens when you use different convex lenses.

You will need: cardboard tube, thin card stock, tape, scissors, sharp pencil, tracing paper.

Camera lenses
Some camera lenses consist of several lenses, or elements. As rays of light pass through a lens, they are refracted (bent) at different angles. These rays can distort, resulting in multi-colored edges on your print. Multiple-element lenses, like the ones seen here, help to prevent the light rays from distorting.

ZOOMING IN AND OUT

1 Cover one end of a cardboard tube with thin card stock and tape it down. Pierce a small hole in the center with a sharp pencil.

2 Wrap a large square of card stock around the other end of the tube. Tape the edge down to form another tube that slides over the first.

3 Cut a circle of tracing paper big enough to stick over the end of your sliding tube. Tape it firmly in place. This is your focal plane.

Record what you see through your zoom lens. Slide the tubes in and out to make the image bigger (left) or smaller (below)

4 Aim the tube at a window or bright light (with the tracing paper end at your eye). Hold it right up to your eye to get it level with your line of sight, and then hold it at least 4–6 in. away from your eye. You should now see an image on the tracing paper screen.

Flat and curved mirrors

Some cameras have one or more mirrors instead of a lens. All the rays that hit a mirror are reflected. A flat mirror *(right)* reflects all rays in the same way, so your image looks unchanged (although left and right seem reversed).

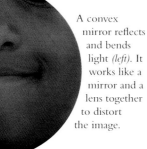

A convex mirror reflects and bends light *(left)*. It works like a mirror and a lens together to distort the image.

Simple close-ups

Put a small object, such as a coin, on a flat surface. Hold a magnifying glass (the larger, the better) in front of the viewfinder and move the camera until the coin fills about a quarter of the frame. Put the magnifying glass in front of the camera lens and take the photograph. Take a few more shots with the camera a little closer and then try moving the camera a little farther away. A macro lens can be attached to a camera to take close-ups, and some have a mini-macro lens attached permanently.

LIGHTING AND FLASH

Lighting is one of the most important parts of photography. The kind of light you take your picture in, how that light hits the subject, and where you take the picture from, all affect the results. Outdoors, most photos are taken with natural light. Artificial light is needed indoors, or outdoors when there is not enough natural light. Photographs can be taken in dim natural light without additional artificial light, but only with very long exposures. Lighting can also create dramatic effects. Flash lighting makes a very bright light for a fraction of a second. Most small cameras have a small, built-in flash unit.

Lights and reflectors

Photographic studios have lots of strong lights. They allow the photographer to create many different lighting effects, without worrying about natural light. Some lights make light over a wide area, others make narrow beams. Using umbrellas and sheets of reflecting material can direct the light, too. These can be used to help reduce the contrast on bright sunny days.

With frontlighting, light is coming to the subject from the same direction as the camera position or slightly above. It lights the subject evenly, but gives a flat look because there are no strong shadows or highlights.

Backlighting means that the subject is between the light and the camera. It can make your subject look darker. The light does not have to be directly behind. Here, two lights have been set at a 45° angle behind the subject, one on either side.

If a picture is side-lit from the back, then the light is coming across your subject. Sidelighting will often give the most interesting or dramatic photographs, because it creates shadows that give more shape and depth to the subject.

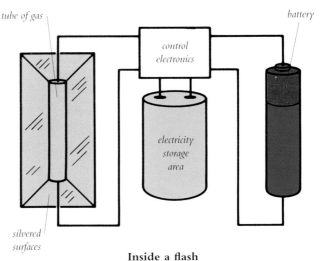

tube of gas

battery

control electronics

electricity storage area

silvered surfaces

Light in a flash

Light from a flash unit only lasts for a fraction of a second. It is carefully timed to flash when the camera's shutter is open. Many cameras have a built-in flash unit. A more powerful flash gun can be added to an SLR camera (above). Most cameras have a signal that tells you when you need to use the flash.

Inside a flash

Flash (above) is made by sending a very large electric current through a narrow tube of gas. This makes a lightning-like flash. The flash's batteries gradually build up a storage area of electric charge, which is released very quickly. It is like filling a pitcher from a dripping tap and then pouring all the water out at once, or blowing up a balloon and then bursting it.

Bouncing and diffusing

Direct flash from the camera to the subject can cause harsh shadows and red-eye (where the flash creates red reflections in a person's eyes). Bounce flash means aiming the flash at the ceiling, so that the light spreads out. Some photographers diffuse flash with a sheet of material attached to the top of the flash, as on the right.

These people are sitting at different distances from the flash. This means that some of them are overexposed (have too much light), while others are underexposed.

Arrange people so that they are all about the same distance from the camera. This should ensure that everyone is properly exposed.

WORKING WITH LIGHT

Red-eye is caused by light from a flash unit near the camera lens bouncing off the retina (at the back of the eye) and back into the lens. With SLR cameras, the flash can be moved to one side to avoid red-eye.

Y ou can improve many of your photographs by giving thought to the lighting before you shoot. For pictures of people, try some of the simple suggestions here. If you're taking pictures outside, move around your subject to study the effects of light as it falls at different angles. You can also ask people you are photographing to tilt their heads at different angles, so that the sunlight lights up their faces. If there isn't enough light, some cameras have a backlight button that lengthens the exposure time for dark subjects. You could also use flash to light up the darker areas. This is known as using fill-in flash.

CREATING LIGHTING EFFECTS

You will need: a camera, large sheets of white and colored paper or card stock, aluminum foil, desk lamp, flashlight, colored tissue paper.

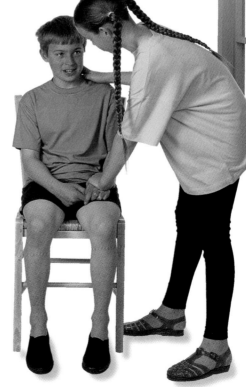

1 Sit your subject near a window and ask them to turn their head in different positions. Move around the room to see the effects of front-, side- and backlighting.

2 Hold a sheet of white paper or card stock near your subject to reflect some light from the window back onto their face. The reflected light fills in the shadows caused by the sidelighting. Do the same with colored paper. This will add color to your subject's face.

3 Try the same with aluminum foil or a piece of shiny card stock. See how this gives a much brighter reflected light. Crushing the foil and then smoothing it out again will diffuse the light in interesting and creative ways.

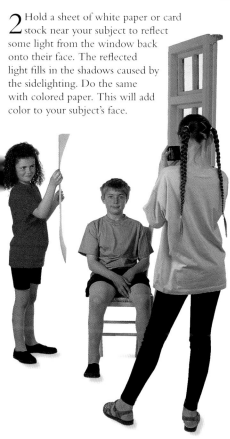

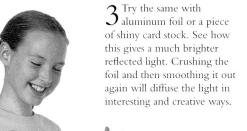

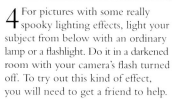

4 For pictures with some really spooky lighting effects, light your subject from below with an ordinary lamp or a flashlight. Do it in a darkened room with your camera's flash turned off. To try out this kind of effect, you will need to get a friend to help.

5 To take this approach even further, experiment with putting your hand in front of the light. As with the previous step, turn off your camera's flash if you can, and hold the camera very still. If you have a tripod, use that to free your hands.

6 For less harsh lighting, put a sheet of tissue paper in front of the lamp or flashlight. Try this with colored tissue paper to see what effects you can achieve. You can also take flash photos with a small piece of tissue paper over the flash unit.

USING FILTERS

A photographic filter changes the light as it enters the camera's lens. There are hundreds of different filters, and each one creates its own effect. The most common filter is called a skylight filter. It lets all visible light through the lens but stops invisible ultraviolet light from getting in, as ultraviolet light can make photographs look unnaturally blue. Filters called graduate filters make some parts of the scene darker. They are often used to darken very bright skies. Colored filters, such as red or yellow, can make black-and-white photographs look very dramatic. There are other special-effect filters that you can buy for adding different effects to your photographs. Smearing petroleum jelly on the edges of a clear filter can give a photograph a soft effect.

Normally filters are only used on SLR cameras. Some filters are circular, and screw onto the end of the camera's lens. Others are designed to slot into a filter holder at the front of the lens.

Bright lights
You will not always want strong reflections and bright light in a picture *(right)*.

Polarizing filter
Here *(left)*, putting a polarizing filter in front of the lens has made the reflections and strong light disappear. These filters cut out certain light rays from a scene, but let others through. They can also have a dramatic effect on skies, making them a much darker blue. If you want to take pictures through a window, a polarizing filter will reduce reflections in the glass.

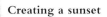

Creating a sunset

With a sunset filter, you can turn a daytime sky *(left)* into a beautiful sunset *(below)*. Half the filter is clear and the other half has a slight orange tint. Position the tint at the top of your shot and the sky appears reddish.

Making your own

You can make filters from transparent, colored candy wrappers. Put clean wrappers in front of the viewfinder to see what effect they have. Then attach them to the front of the lens with small pieces of tape.

Interesting shapes

A frame filter is a black mask with a shape cut in it. This makes the scene you are shooting come out in that shape. The other parts of the scene will be black. Frame filters come in simple shapes, such as squares and ovals, and more complex shapes, such as keyholes. Shooting through holes in walls or old trees can give you the same creative effects.

USEFUL TIPS

Here are a few simple tips that should help you to improve your photographic technique and avoid some common mistakes. Good technique is made up of technical skill and an eye for an interesting subject. Remember that a complicated SLR camera does not necessarily take the best photographs, and that great shots are perfectly possible with a simple point-and-shoot camera. The first thing to decide is the type of film you want to use (color print, color slide or black-and-white). Always load and unload your film in dim lighting. Once it has all been exposed, place it in its container and get it processed as soon as possible.

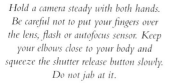

Hold a camera steady with both hands. Be careful not to put your fingers over the lens, flash or autofocus sensor. Keep your elbows close to your body and squeeze the shutter release button slowly. Do not jab at it.

Check the background
When you are taking portraits, or photographs of groups of people, always look at the background as well as at your subject. If necessary, recompose your picture to avoid the sort of accident that has happened in this shot. Many cameras have a portrait setting that gives a shallow depth of field. This automatically makes the background go out of focus.

Fill the frame
Do not be afraid to get close to your subject. For example, if you are taking a portrait, make sure the person's head and shoulders fill the frame *(right)*. But be careful not to get too close, because the camera may not be able to focus *(far right)*. If you get too close with an autofocus camera, it will not let you take a picture.

Natural frames

Try adding some interest to photos by shooting through archways or doors to frame the subject. With photos of groups or scenery, you can include overhanging branches in the foreground.

The rule of thirds

Try using the rule of thirds: place the subject a third of the way across or up or down the frame. This makes the shot more interesting. With autofocus cameras, you often have to use your focus lock to point at the subject first and then recompose the picture before shooting. Try this with landscapes—for example, having a mountain range in the top third of the frame.

A different viewpoint

Photographs taken from a standing position have the same viewpoint as your eyes usually do. Changing the camera's viewpoint can give more interesting results. Try kneeling, or even lying down.

Bad weather photographs

You do not always need to wait for good weather before taking photos. In fact, overhead sunshine tends to give flat, dull pictures. Stormy clouds can be much more interesting than cloudless skies. Remember to protect your camera in extreme weather conditions to make sure it stays dry.

SPECIAL PHOTOGRAPHY

M ost cameras and lenses are designed for general photography. However, there are some types of camera that take photographs in unusual formats or in special conditions. For example, you can use certain cameras to take really wide panoramic views, or to shoot scenes entirely underwater. It is also possible to take pictures inside the human body with an attachment called an endoscope. There are also some unusual types of film. Some produce odd colors or shades in your photographs. Another type of film records technical information about each shot, while self-processing film does not have to be developed.

Disposable underwater cameras can take photographs while completely submerged. The camera's body is recycled after the film is processed.

Underwater SLRs

Divers take photographs underwater with special SLR cameras that are waterproof even when they are many feet down. They can also withstand the high pressure of being in deep water. Special housings are available for many cameras to enable land cameras to be used underwater or in adverse conditions such as during a cave diving or pot-holing expedition.

If you want to photograph anything deep down in the sea, you need to use extremely bright lights.

Spacious photographs

Panoramic cameras can take very wide photographs, which are good for shots of large groups of people or landscapes. Many compact cameras take pictures that are called panoramic, but they actually only appear to be so. They are no wider than a standard frame, just shorter, to help you compose your shot.

FACT BOX

• Certain cameras are able to decide themselves whether a scene is a portrait, a landscape or an action shot, and adjust the aperture and shutter to suit the photograph.

• APS film is similar to 35-mm film. It records information, such as the exposure settings and frame size, on a special magnetic layer and this is used during processing.

• You can buy disposable panoramic cameras.

Laser photographs

A hologram is a three-dimensional (3-D) picture that looks 3-D no matter what angle you look at it from. The picture changes as you move your head from side to side. However, holograms are not taken with a camera. Another kind of equipment is used to record how laser light bounces off the subject from different directions.

Advanced systems

Many new compact cameras (and some SLRs) work according to the APS, or the Advanced Photographic System. They allow you to set the frame size for each shot individually and even to change film rolls midway without damage.

AMAZING EFFECTS

Discover how to take stereo photos and how to get an amazing three-dimensional effect from them. It is easier than you might think, and you can do it with the most basic compact camera. Simply take two photos of the same scene from different angles. When they have been developed, place them side by side to see the three-dimensional effect for yourself. The effect works because, like many animals, humans have binocular vision. This means that the two different views from our two eyes overlap. In the overlapping area, our eyes see slightly different views, which makes things appear in three dimensions. Once you have tried this experiment, you can to find out how to construct a grand panoramic picture by taking a series of photos of the same scene.

Place your pair of stereo photographs side by side to view them.

The diagram on the right shows how the stereo effect is created—because our two eyes see slightly different views.

left eye sees this view

right eye sees this view

the actual 3-D box you are looking at

MAKE YOUR MODEL COME ALIVE

MATERIALS

You will need: camera, model.

1 Choose a simple object such as this model of a toy. Holding the camera very steady, take a picture. Try to include a little space around your subject.

2 Take a step about 8 in. to your left, and take another photo. Try taking more pairs of photographs, using different distances between the two photographs.

3 Put your pictures down side by side on a flat surface. Stand over them and place your index finger between the two. With your eyes directly above the photos, look down at the finger and slowly raise it toward your nose, keeping it in focus. The two images you see below should merge into one 3-D image.

Make a panorama

Choose a good general landscape scene, with no close-up objects in it. Now, using a camera lens set at 35 or 50 mm, take a series of photographs that overlap slightly. Start by looking toward your left and move your head slightly around to the right for each of the following shots. When your prints are developed, lay them out in the right order to recreate your scene. When you are happy with the arrangement, tape them together carefully.

This completed panorama (above) works well because it is a simple, open scene. If it had been filled with small objects, then the effect might not have been as good. If you want people in your scene, try to keep them away from areas that will overlap in the finished panorama. On the other hand, you could ask a friend to move into different parts of the scene for each different shot and produce a picture with multiple images of him or her.

MOVING PICTURES

A movie camera is used to take moving pictures. It takes a whole series of photographs in quick succession (usually about 25 every second), on a very long roll of film. Any moving object appears in a slightly different position in each frame. When the photographs are displayed quickly, one after the other, the movement in the original scene appears to be recreated. The films are usually transparency, or positive rather than negative. The films are put into a projector to be shown. Today, movie cameras are used mainly for professional movie-making. Home movie cameras used to be very popular, but today they have been replaced by video cameras.

Moving pictures rely on the fact that we have persistence of vision. This means our eyes remember a picture for a split second. To see how this works, look at a scene and close your eyes quickly.

Recording motion

The first movie cameras grew out of experiments to record and study animal motion rather than for entertainment. This sequence *(left)* was taken by British photographer Eadweard Muybridge (1830–1904). He had first come up with the idea of moving pictures in 1877 after taking a series of photographs of a horse running, using 24 different cameras. Muybridge produced hundreds of images recording the complex movements of animals and humans that were too quick for the unaided human eye to follow. Artists used his pictures as reference for their paintings.

Movie film

This is just like the rolls of film you put in a stills, or ordinary, camera. In fact, 35-mm film was originally made for movie cameras. The image in each frame of the film is slightly different than the one before.

Electronic images

Unlike the film used in movie and ordinary cameras, video cameras use tape with a magnetic coating. It does not record the amount of light in a scene; instead, pictures are recorded by an electronic signal that distorts the tape. The video player reads this signal and reproduces the image.

Inside a movie camera

A movie camera has similar parts to an ordinary camera—a lens, shutter and aperture. It also has some extra parts for taking photos in quick succession. The film is wound on, ready for the next frame, while the shutter is closed. The shutter speed is always the same and the exposure is controlled just by the aperture.

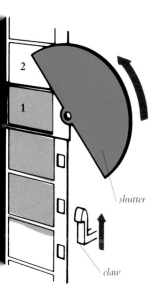

shutter

claw

shutter open, first frame exposed

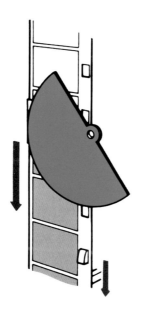

shutter closed, claw pulls film down

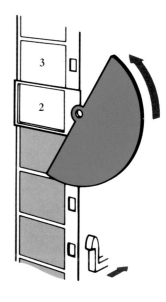

shutter open, second frame exposed

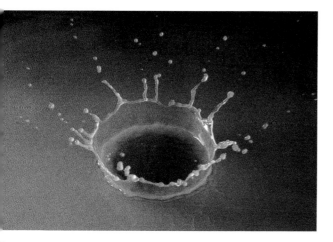

High-speed photos

This is a frame from a high-speed film. Some movie cameras can take hundreds, or even thousands, of photographs every second. When they are played back at normal speed, the action is slowed right down.

FACT BOX

• The world's fastest movie cameras are used by scientists. They can take 600 million frames every second.

• If you used a movie camera like this to film a bullet fired from a gun, the bullet would take 1,000 frames to move just one millimeter.

• Like normal camera film, movie camera film comes in different formats. Professionals on location shoots tend to use 16-mm format.

• In an IMAX cinema, the screen is as high as seven elephants sitting on top of each other.

• On IMAX film, the frames are four times larger than 35-mm film.

ANIMATION

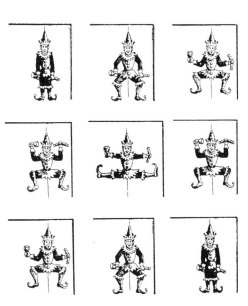

A nimation is making inanimate objects, or objects that cannot move by themselves, appear to move. Frames of the film are photographed one at a time with a special movie camera, although you can create animation using video cameras. Between each frame, the objects are moved slightly. Sometimes this is combined with camera movement or zoom effects. When the finished film is viewed, the objects seem to move. Some animated objects are models, which are photographed to make animated movies. Others are drawings, which are photographed to make cartoons. Modern cartoon animation is often done by computer, so the photography stage is not needed. Quite often only the main drawings are made by an artist, and a computer plans the movements and frames using animation software.

Photo flick-book
The simplest way of making moving pictures is to put all the frames into a book and flip through the pages. In the early 1800s, flick-books of photographs (called filoscopes) were used to entertain children as movies had not yet been invented. You can see some of the pages from an old filoscope above.

Turning marvel
A thaumotrope is a double-sided disk, often made of cardboard, which has partial pictures on either side. When you spin the disk, the pictures appear to merge. So, if you had a bird on one side and a cage on the other, when the disk was spun you would see the bird in the cage. The name "thaumotrope" comes from the Greek words for marvel and turning.

This picture shows a scene from one of the popular Wallace and Gromit films, made by Aardman Animations Ltd. Model animation is a highly skillful and time-consuming job. The models must be moved very, very slightly between each frame. There are about 25 frames for every second of film.

FACT BOX

• A movie camera used for shooting cels is secured so that it looks down on a flat baseboard. The cels for one frame are placed on the board and a photo is taken. Then the cels for the next frame are shot, and so on.

• Model animation is done with a camera, held firm on a rostrum, or platform, so that it does not shift between frames. However, it can be tilted, panned (moved to follow a moving object) and zoomed to create different effects.

• A 20-minute animated film uses between 15,000 and 30,000 frames.

This picture appears in the top right-hand corner of every other page in this book. Flip all the pages of the book quickly and watch the pictures. What can you see happening?

Enjoying animation

Producing animated children's films is big business. Many cartoons are made with the aid of computers. Some computer packages do all the time-consuming drawing and painting. They can also produce complex, three-dimensional characters, or add cartoon elements to film of real actors. In special effects scenes, real actors may be replaced by computer-generated images of themselves.

Cartoon cels

Until the 1980s, cartoons were made by photographing a series of drawings. The drawings were done on transparent plastic sheets called cels. Moving characters were drawn on one cel and the still background on another, to prevent having to draw the background again and again for each frame. Once the cels were completed, they were photographed with a movie camera. When these were shown in rapid succession, a moving film appeared.

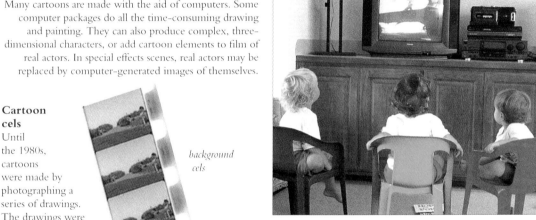

background cels

character cels (notice how each one is different either in expression or the clothing)

EASY ANIMATION

During the 1800s, there was a craze for optical toys, such as flick-books. Many of them created an illusion of movement by displaying a sequence of pictures in quick succession. At first, the pictures were hand-drawn. Later, photos taken by early movie cameras were used as well. Here, you can find out how to make a toy called a phenakistoscope, and how to use it to turn a series of pictures into animation. Our toy is slightly different from the Victorian one on the right, as it has slots cut around the edges, rather than in the center.

A phenakistoscope (above) was an early device used to view moving pictures in a mirror. It held a set of images that were all slightly different. When you spun the disk, you saw an action sequence through the slots.

A series of simple drawings works best. This strip of images is for a zoetrope.

You will need: thick, dark-colored card stock, sharp pencil, ruler, scissors, paper, dark felt-tip marker, tape, camera, models.

MAKE YOUR OWN PHENAKISTOSCOPE

1 On a piece of thick card stock, draw a circle measuring 10 in. across. Divide it into eight equal segments. At the end of each segment line, draw slots 2 in. long and ¼ in. wide.

2 Now cut out your disk, and the evenly spaced slots around the outside of it. Make sure that the slots are no wider than ¼ in. These will be your viewing holes.

3 On pieces of light-colored paper, draw a series of eight pictures. These should form a sequence of movements. Make sure that your drawings are fairly simple and clear, and that they are drawn with clean, strong lines.

4 Attach the little drawings to the disk by taping them just under the slots. You may need to cut them to fit, but make sure the picture is centered below the slot. Push a pencil through the center of the card stock disk to make a handle.

5 Stand in front of a mirror. Hold the disk vertically, with the pictures toward the mirror. Spin the disk and look through the slots. You should see an animated loop of action in the mirror.

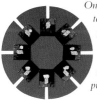

Once you have mastered the technique of making a photo phenakistoscope, you can get more adventurous with your subjects and story lines. Try adding more models or props—for example, putting hats on the models.

PHOTO PHENAKISTOSCOPE

1 Now try a model animation. Take eight photographs of a model from the same position (use a tripod if you can). Move the model(s) slightly each time. The models should take up the middle third of the photograph frame.

2 Cut your photos to size and stick them to the phenakistoscope, one under each slot. Your phenakistoscope will work better if the photos have a dark frame, or you can just cover the edges roughly with a black felt-tip marker pen.

A zoetrope
This zoetrope from the 1860s was used to display long strips of drawings showing simple action sequences. They were placed inside a cylinder that could be rotated by hand. The moving pictures were then viewed through the vertical slots cut in the cylinder.

CAMERAS IN SCIENCE

Some advanced microscopes (above) can take very detailed close-up photos. You can also do the same thing with a normal microscope, by fitting an SLR camera to it. You remove the SLR's lens, and the microscope acts as a close-up lens for the camera.

Most of us use our cameras for recording special occasions, and when traveling, or for taking pictures of our friends. Photography is also extremely important in science and technology. For example, it is used for recording images that have been made by scientific instruments, so that they can be studied later. It is also used to record experiments that happen too fast for the human eye to see, and for analyzing experimental results. In many modern scientific instruments, electronic cameras have taken the place of film cameras. Their images can be transferred easily to computers for analysis.

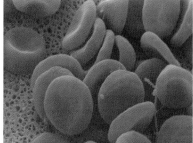

Microscope photographs
A photograph that is taken with a microscope is called a photomicrograph. This one is a close-up of the red blood cells in our blood.

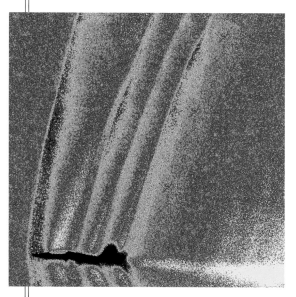

Recording speed on camera
This type of photograph is known as a schlieren photograph. It shows the shock waves around a T-38 aircraft flying at great speed—1.1 times the speed of sound, or Mach 1.1. The waves appear as red and green diagonal lines in the photograph. It enables scientists to see that the main shock waves come from the nose and tail of the plane. Smaller shock waves come from the engine inlets and wings. The yellow stream behind the aircraft is caused by the exhaust of the jet engine.

Photographing heat
All objects give off heat rays called infrared rays. Hotter objects give off stronger rays. A special type of film called infrared film is sensitive to heat rays rather than light rays. Hot and cold objects show up in different colors or shades.

When you are taking photos of the sky with a telescope using long exposures, the telescope often has to move slowly across the sky. This is to prevent the stars from becoming streaks on your prints. This happens because the Earth and stars are slowly moving. It is like taking a picture of a traffic light from a moving car. The lights would appear streaked.

Capturing the stars

Just as a camera can be added to a microscope to take close-up pictures, one can also be added to a telescope. The telescope acts like a very powerful telephoto lens for the camera. (A telephoto lens makes distant objects seem much closer.) Light from the stars is very weak, and so long exposures are needed.

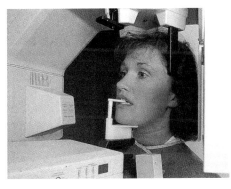

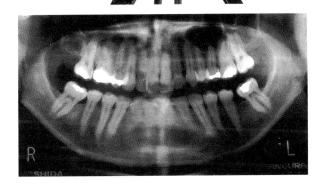

Where more X-rays reach the film, through soft parts of the body, the film turns a darker tone when it is developed. Bones and teeth show up white.

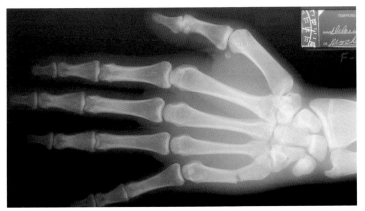

Taking X-ray pictures

X-rays are used to photograph inside bodies. Unlike light rays, X-rays can pass though the soft parts of your body—skin and muscle. X-ray film is simply processed to produce negatives not prints. X-rays help dentists or doctors to find out all kinds of things about the body. The picture on the left shows the hand of a boxer with a fractured finger caused through punching. Other kinds of X-ray technology are used to scan for faults in the structure of buildings or aircraft, enabling repairs to take place before a part fails or causes an accident.

CAMERAS AND COMPUTERS

Just like ordinary cameras, digital cameras come as compacts and SLRs. They have a lens and shutter, but, in the space where the film would normally be, they have a light-sensitive microchip. This means that the photographs are stored in the camera's memory.

Photographs are often used in computer applications. For example, a multimedia CD-ROM about nature might contain thousands of photographs of animals and plants. Photographs stored and displayed by computer are called digital images because they consist of a long series of numbers as opposed to being a physical print on paper. Digital images are either prints that have been scanned into a computer to turn them into digital form, or images that have been photographed with a digital, filmless, camera. Digital images can be copied over and over again, without any loss in quality. This means that they can be sent easily from one computer to another—over the Internet, for example.

FACT BOX
• The highest resolution digital cameras divide a picture into a grid about 7,000 pixels (dots) wide and 5,000 pixels deep.

• Many digital pictures use 24-bit color. This means that each pixel can be any one of 16,771,216 different colors.

Video phone
The digital video camera on top of this computer *(above)* takes pictures that are sent down the telephone line and appear on another computer's screen. This lets the people at both computers see each other.

Floppy disk camera
The digital camera on the right uses a normal floppy disk that can be placed directly into a computer. The pictures can then be worked on using computer software.

Pixel pictures

A digital image is made up of pixels, or dots. A number represents the color of each tiny dot. High-resolution (sharper) images divide the picture into a greater number of smaller dots than low-resolution ones, but they take up more computer memory.

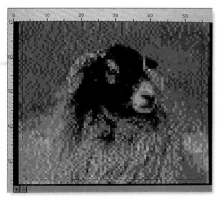

Retouching

Once a photo is digitized, it can be altered in any way by the computer. For example, colors can be changed or another photo can be added in. A polar bear could be put in a desert! It is much easier than trying the same thing with normal photography.

Morphing

Many films and television programs make use of computer-manipulated photographs and film images to create stunning special effects. Morphing, for example, is where a person or object changes into something or someone else slowly, on screen. To achieve this, the computer software gradually merges two totally different images together.

This shows a digitized picture on a computer screen before it has been manipulated.

Here is the same picture after it has been manipulated by computer. Can you see how it has changed?

GLOSSARY

aperture
In most cameras the aperture is a hole behind the lens that can be adjusted to let more or less light onto the film.

APS (Advanced Photographic System) camera
Camera that allows you to change the format for individual shots.

autofocus
A feature on a camera that automatically adjusts the lens position to make sure a scene is in focus.

camera obscura
A darkened box or room in which images of outside objects are projected.

converging (or convex) lens
A lens which curves outward, as on a magnifying glass. This causes light rays from an object to bend inward toward each other and makes things seem larger.

conversion filter
A filter that can be attached to a camera to produce a natural lighting effect when you are taking pictures indoors.

depth of field
The distance between the nearest and farthest parts of the scene that are in focus at one time.

diffraction
The scattering of light rays.

diffuser
A filter, similar to a sheet of tissue paper, than can be attached to a camera to soften light from a flash.

digital camera
A camera that takes electronic images that are downloaded onto a computer to be viewed.

diverging lens
Lens that causes light rays to spread outward.

endoscope
A long, slender camera attachment that goes inside the body to take pictures of internal organs relaying the images to a computer screen.

exposures
Photographs on film.

exposure time
The time it takes for the camera to take a picture. This is the time a shutter is open letting light from the scene hit the lens.

fill-in flash
Using the flash to light up certain areas of your picture, but leaving natural light in the background.

filter
Transparent material attached to a lens that alters the color of the light or the way the light rays pass through it.

fish-eye lens
A very wide-angle lens that collects light from 180 degrees. The center of the scene looks much bigger.

flash
A bulb attached to the camera that provides a quick burst of light so that a picture can be taken in darkness.

focal length
The distance between the center of a lens and the focal point—the point where light rays enter.

focal plane
The area at the back of a camera where the exposed film is held flat. It is the point at which the light rays meet.

focus
A camera is in focus when the light rays from an object meet on the focal plane to form a sharp image of the scene.

format
The size and shape of a print and the way it can be viewed (as a print, a slide or on a computer, for example).

frame
The area seen through the viewfinder.

frame filter
Black material with a hole cut in the middle, such as a keyhole or circle, that fits over the lens. The scene will come out inside that shape on the print, and the covered area will be black.

infrared light
Rays of light that are invisible because they have a wavelength that is longer than the red end of the part of the light spectrum we can see.

ISO (International Standards Organization) rating
International rating system for film that tells you their speed. An ISO 200 film is twice as fast as an ISO 100.

laser light
A narrow and powerful beam of light produced by a laser machine, used in making holograms, video disks and cutting equipment, among other things.

latent image
Invisible image produced by light hitting the silver crystals in the film.

leaf shutter
A shutter that is made up of a number of overlapping plates that retract to open.

lens
A transparent material that is curved on one or both sides. It bends rays of light and directs them onto the film.

light spectrum
The colors that light can be split into. The light spectrum is part of the electromagnetic spectrum that includes light rays, sound rays, microwaves, radio waves, X-rays and Gamma rays.

macro lens
A close-up lens that has very short focal length, used to take pictures of objects very close to the camera.

monochrome
Black-and-white film or photographic paper, it shows colors as shades of black /gray.

negative
The photographic image on the developed film from which prints will be made. The colors or tones are reversed, so dark areas look light and light areas look dark.

overexposure
Where the subject of a photograph appears dark. It is caused by not enough light rays from the subject hitting the film.

panning
Moving a camera to follow a moving subject.

panoramic picture
A photograph showing an extra wide view of a scene such as a landscape.

pixels
Tiny dots that make up a digital image.

polarizing filter
A filter put in front of a lens to cut out reflections from water, glass or metal.

Polaroid camera
A type of camera that can take and develop individual prints immediately as it has developing chemicals inside.

positive
A print or slide showing a photographic image with colors or tones that are the same as in the original scene.

primary colors
Three colors—red, blue and green or cyan, magenta and yellow. When combined, they make any other color.

prism
Specially shaped glass used to split white light into the spectrum, or to reflect light rays away from their normal path.

reflectors
A sheet of reflecting material or umbrella used to light a subject.

refraction
The bending of light rays.

reversal film or slide film
A film that when developed gives a positive image, known as a transparency.

rostrum
A platform used to hold a film or video camera still during shooting.

shutter
Camera mechanism, like a little door, which opens and shuts to control the amount of time that light is allowed to fall onto the lens.

SLR (Single Lens Reflex)
A design of camera that allows you to see exactly what the lens sees.

still photography
Normal photography showing a single image (as opposed to taking moving images with a movie camera).

telephoto lens
A lens that takes a close-up picture of a distant scene.

tripod
A camera stand with three legs.

tungsten film
Film designed to be used inside. It reproduces light from a lamp or indoor light as if it was white, so the pictures do not look yellowy.

ultraviolet light
Rays of light that are invisible to our eyes because they have a wavelength that is shorter than the blue end of the part of the light spectrum we can see.

underexposure
A photograph that looks washed out as too much light from the subject has hit the film.

viewfinder
The window you look through to see what will be in your photograph.

wide-angle lens
Lens with an angle of view that is wider than normal for the human eye.

X-ray photographs
Pictures taken of the inside of our bodies, used to show broken bones.

zoom lens
A lens with a variable focal length, so that you can alter it to get in close to a distant subject or use as a normal lens.

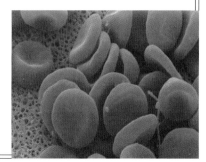

Index

Acknowledgments
b=bottom, t=top
c=center, l=left, r=right

Aardman Animations Ltd:
54br. Mary Evans: 4bl,
52cl. Galaxy Picture
Library /Tim Grabham:
59tr. Holt Studios
International: 37tl & tr,
53bl, /Nigel Cattlin: 55br,
58br, 61tl. Robin Kerrod:
59tl. Microscopix: 58r.
Oxford Scientific Films
/Scott Camazine: 59bl,
/Laurence Gould: 48cr.
Chris Oxlade: 47tr. The
Projection Box: 54tl, 56tr.
Science & Society: 9c,
33tr, 54bl, 57br. Science
Photo Library : 58bl,
/George Bernard: 59cl,
/Phillipe Plailly: 49bl,
/Francoise Sauze:59cr,
/Sinclair Stammers: 58tl.
Robert Scott Associates:
11tr, 49br. Sony: 60br.
Tony Stone Images: 55cr.
Lucy Tizard: 42tl.
Zefa/Powerstock: 5bl &
br, 34bl, 47bl, 48bl, 49t.